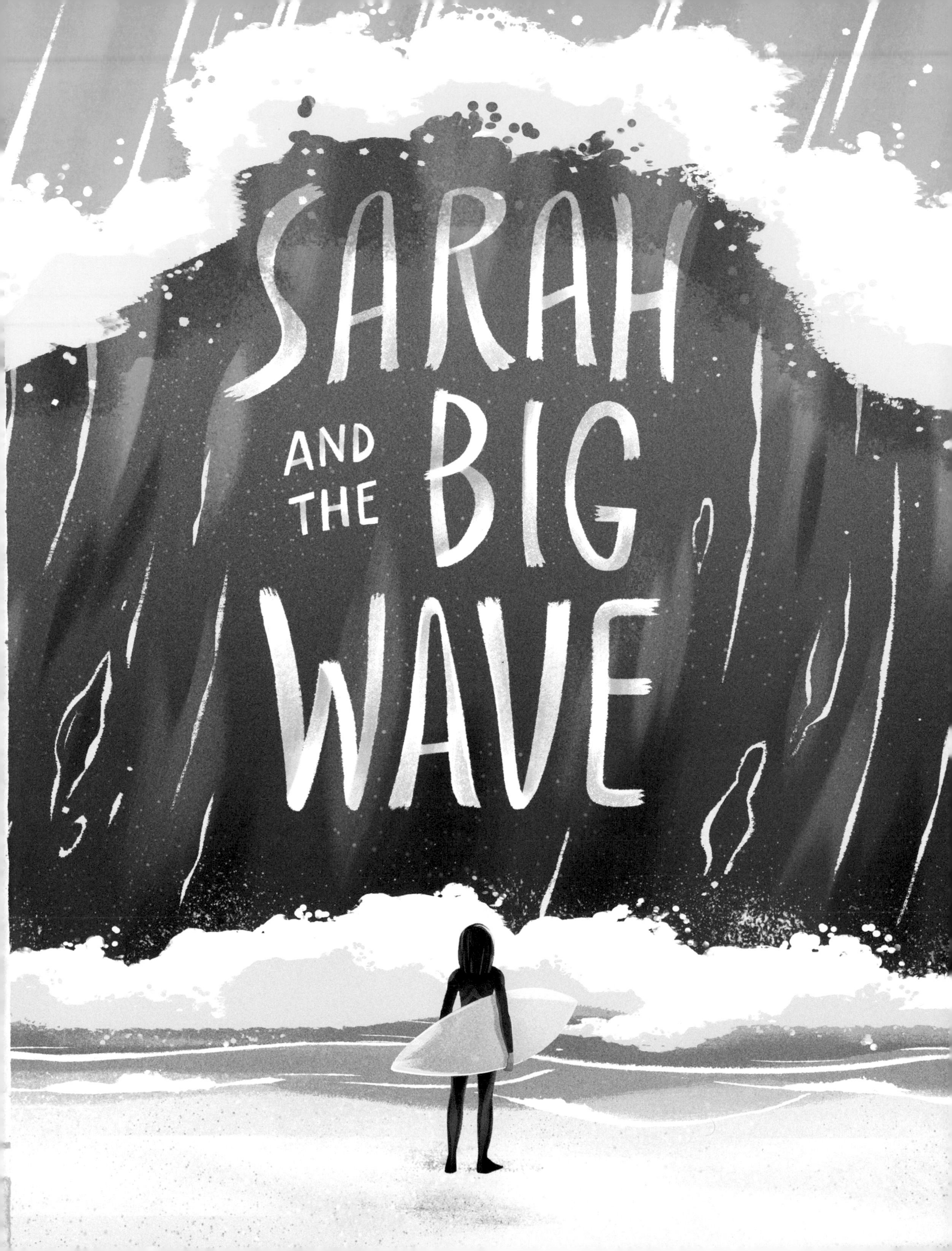
SARAH
AND THE BIG
WAVE

Henry Holt and Company, Publishers since 1866
Henry Holt® is a registered trademark of Macmillan Publishing Group, LLC.
120 Broadway, New York, NY 10271

mackids.com

Library of Congress Cataloging-in-Publication Data is available.
ISBN 978-1-250-23948-8

Our books may be purchased in bulk for promotional, educational, or business use.
Please contact your local bookseller or the Macmillan Corporate and Premium Sales Department
at (800) 221-7945 ext. 5442 or by email at MacmillanSpecialMarkets@macmillan.com.

First Edition, 2021
Printed in China by RR Donnelley Asia Printing Solutions Ltd., Dongguan City, Guangdong Province

The illustrations for this book were created digitally.

10 9 8 7 6 5 4 3 2 1

SARAH
AND THE BIG
WAVE

The True Story of the First Woman to Surf Mavericks

Written by **BONNIE TSUI**

Illustrated by **SOPHIE DIAO**

Henry Holt and Company • New

IT'S A COLD, bright February day in California, and Sarah is in the ocean, waiting for her big wave.

Sarah is a surfer.

Two thousand miles away, in the middle of the Pacific Ocean, her wave was born in a winter storm. It has taken more than a week for the wave to get from where it began to where Sarah is today, waiting.

Storms that form in the North Pacific often follow the jet stream, gathering power and energy as they send high seas straight for the California coast.

In a way, Sarah has been waiting all her life for this wave. She began surfing when she was young, in California and Hawaii, where she grew up.

At first, the waves she surfed were little waves.

Then she tried medium waves.

And then she tried big waves.

She found she loved the big ones best.

Bigger waves, though, meant bigger breaths when she fell and went underwater. Sometimes the waves held Sarah down for what seemed to be a long time, but she learned to stay calm by counting . . .

1 . . .

2 . . .

3 . . .

4 . . .

5...

sometimes as long as forty-five seconds until she popped
up to the surface again. Counting made her realize that she
always had more breath than she thought.

The North Shore of Oahu is famous for big waves. What's a big wave? Usually it's a wave that's twenty, thirty, forty, even *fifty feet tall or more*. A fifty-foot wave: That's pretty tall.

That's a five-story building.

Sarah is a little bit scared, but she's also excited. When she started surfing in Hawaii, she was the only girl out there.

At first she didn't have anyone to surf with. The boys didn't want to hang out with her. The girls didn't want to go surf.

People told her, "Girls aren't supposed to be in the water."

That didn't stop her.

Because not many girls were surfing then, she had a hard time finding the right equipment: the right size surfboard, the right size clothing. She had to wear men's wet suits and surf shorts.

too big,

Too wide,

too narrow.

Nothing fit right.

Eventually, Sarah met a circle of surfers who treated her
love of surfing with respect and friendship. They became very
good friends.

"Want to surf big waves with us?" they asked.
"Let's do it!" she said. One of them was a surfboard shaper;
he made boards that were just right for her to surf big waves.

She ended up marrying one of those friends.

His name is Mike.

Sarah and Mike moved to California from Hawaii. Near their new home was a famous big-wave surf break called Mavericks.

Mavericks is known for being big, cold, and intimidating. In the winter, storms in the North Pacific send swells right up Mavericks's crescent-shaped reef, where the contact can create massive waves of fifty feet or more.

"Mount Everest meets Niagara Falls" is one way surfers describe the monster waves at Mavericks. It's a dangerous place to surf, and even expert big-wave surfers have made mistakes and lost their lives there.

Now, on that cold afternoon in February . . . it is beautiful and sunny: low tide, waves twenty-five to thirty feet high. Before today, Sarah has paddled out to Mavericks on her surfboard, but she has not yet caught a wave. Before today, no woman has yet surfed Mavericks. Today is the day.

The water is dark and cold and silty. It's a long, tiring paddle out to where the wave breaks, and Sarah battles her way past the foamy whitewater.

The wave continues to grow as she drops in;
by the time she's surfed part of the way down, the
wave pulls her backward a bit, a little closer into its
embrace. Then, all of a sudden, it releases her for
the thrilling, hair-raising ride down its face.

It is super cold, terrifying,
exhilarating. And all Sarah can think
as she cruises out of the wave is:
I want to do that again!

Then she sees her wave. What a gorgeous, dark, fierce thing
it is, the horizon rearing up to greet her. She begins to paddle
toward shore to meet the wave as it arrives.

Suddenly, the wave hits
the reef, and she is looking
two, three stories down.
Then she stands.

Past Mushroom Rock to the south and Sail Rock to the north—in between them is the gateway to the surf break. A half mile from shore, she sits up and waits.

For a split second, Sarah hangs in midair . . .

. . . and then she's off,
roaring down the wave at
thirty miles an hour.

And she does,
again and again.

A month later, there is a
photographer on the beach,
watching. He takes her picture.

She is Sarah Gerhardt, the first woman to surf Mavericks.
Sarah Gerhardt, the big-wave surfer.

MILESTONES IN THE HISTORY OF WOMEN AND SURFING

1800s–1900s: Despite the fact that women surfed alongside men in Hawaii for centuries, women are discouraged from surfing after the arrival of Western missionaries in Hawaii in the 1800s. The revival of surfing begins in the early 1900s, with the founding of the Outrigger Surf Club and Jack London's visit to Hawaii. His writings about surfing in Waikiki help popularize its practice as it arrives on the US mainland. But the prejudice against women surfing will extend deep into the mid-twentieth century.

1600s: The oldest-known surfboard—papa he'e nalu, in Hawaiian—belonged to the Hawaiian princess Kaneamuna and dates back to this time. It is discovered in her burial cave on the Big Island of Hawaii in 1905.

1968: Two-time world surf champion Joyce Hoffman is the first woman ever recorded to surf the legendarily heavy Pipeline surf break on the North Shore of Oahu.

1890s: Another Hawaiian princess, Kaiulani, introduces surfing to Europe while studying abroad in England (she reportedly surfed the English Channel at Brighton). After returning home, she surfs often at Waikiki Beach. Her surfboard is preserved in Honolulu's Bishop Museum.

1959: *Gidget*, the first Hollywood surf movie—based on the real-life story of Malibu's Kathy Kohner, first told in a young-adult novel written by her father—ignites surf fever in America and brings the masses to the beach.

1975: Rell Sunn, Hawaii's first female lifeguard and a pioneer longboard surf champion, helps start the first women's professional surf tour. She will be one of the first five women named on the International Surfing Museum's Walk of Fame.

1995: Lisa Andersen, who won four World Championships from 1994 to 1997, becomes the first woman on the cover of *Surfer* magazine. She is also named one of *Sports Illustrated*'s top female athletes of the twentieth century.

2010: Keala Kennelly wins the Nelscott Reef Big Wave Classic, the first-ever women's big-wave surf contest. In 2016, she is the first female surfer invited to the Eddie Aikau Big Wave Invitational. That year, she'll also beat everyone, men included, to win the "Barrel of the Year" award at the World Surf League (WSL) Big Wave Awards.

February 2020: Brazilian big-wave surfer Maya Gabeira, who previously landed a spot in the *Guinness Book of World Records* for the biggest wave ever surfed by a woman, breaks her own world record when she surfs a 73.5-foot wave, the biggest wave surfed by *anyone* during the 2019–2020 winter season.

1999: Sarah Gerhardt is the first woman to surf Mavericks.

August 2016: The International Olympic Committee (IOC) announces that the sport of surfing will make its debut at the 2020 Summer Olympics in Tokyo, Japan.

September 2018: The WSL—the major leagues of international surf competition—announces equal prize money for men and women in all contests held on the professional world championship tour, starting with the 2019 season. The big-wave surfers Bianca Valenti, Paige Alms, Keala Kennelly, and Andrea Moller are instrumental in leading this effort.